LAURIE AND ME

a memoir

Wyatt House books may be ordered through booksellers or by contacting:

WYATT HOUSE PUBLISHING
399 Lakeview Dr. W.
Mobile, Alabama 36695
www.wyattpublishing.com
editor@wyattpublishing.com

Because of the dynamic nature of the Internet, any web address or links contained in this book may have changed since publication and may no longer be valid.

Cover and interior design by: Mark Wyatt

ISBN 13: 978-0-9977422-1-3

Printed in the United States of America

LAURIE
AND
ME

A SPIRITUAL JOURNEY THROUGH GRIEF

a memoir

by

LYNN RAYMER

WHP
Wyatt House Publishing

Mobile, Alabama

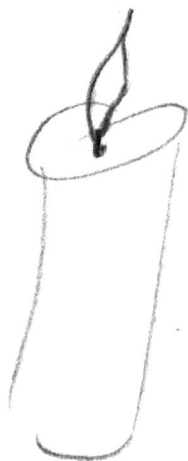

DEDICATION

This book is dedicated to Deborah, Mary and Lucretia, for without their encouragement it would not have happened.

Many thanks to those who took the time to read, edit, and make suggestions. Jean and Jane for editing, Ron, Johnn and Jon for reviewing my use of scripture and my style. And to my family for allowing me to share parts of their story.

Most of all to Larry, for the love and support that he has been to me over the many years of our marriage.

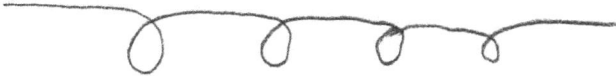

FOREWORD

One evening in August of 2003, I stopped after work for a drink with some of my friends from work. It was the anniversary of my daughter's death 27 years before. As we were sitting there talking, I shared this story with them. Although they knew the basic facts, I had never shared any of the details.

They were touched by the story and suggested that it was a story that needed to be written. It was their feeling that my story could be of help to others going through similar experiences, because they see me as a strong person.

That isn't always how I see myself. I was at first reluctant to even consider writing a book about my grief and spiritual growth. I was afraid that it might do more harm than good.

Everyone grieves in their own way. Reactions are intimate and personal. There is no right or wrong way to mourn the loss of a loved one, especially a child. I write this down, not as a map but as a light at the end of the road. The pain of the loss is still there, so many years later, but it is soft and familiar now.

I picture the process of mourning as a series of loops. At the time of the loss, there is numbness, denial, pain, anger and finally acceptance, not necessarily in that order. As we come to acceptance, life levels out. Then something reminds us of the loss and we go through a loop again. This time we move through the loop a little faster. Each time we are reminded, we move through a loop. Each time it is a little faster, the emotions a little less intense. I still move through a loop as I write this, but it is easier as time goes by. Now I can laugh at some of the memories.

It is my hope that sharing my thoughts, at times being sometimes brutally honest about things I find hard to put into words, will help some other parent struggling with some of the same emotions.

I share my long journey back to God in the hope that my story may help someone else return to God. Faith is also personal and intimate. I do not pretend to have all the answers, only the ones that have helped me.

PRELUDE

Every since I was a child and read I Capture the Castle, by Dodie Smith, which begins "I write this sitting in the kitchen sink", I have wanted to write a book. She captured my imagination. Over the years I have published some small articles on different nursing topics, but never the Great American Novel. Little did I know that one day I would try to write a book with a very different character.

When Larry and I began to talk about marriage after having met only a week before, we knew little about each other but we knew that we belonged together. Our backgrounds were similar in some ways, worlds apart in others.

We came from families where marriage was for life, divorce didn't happen, and children were a natural outcome of marriage. We came from families where faith was an integral part of life. We came from working class families with stay-at-home Moms. And there the similarities ended.

Our life styles had been very different. Larry had grown up in a small trailer home, sharing a room with his sister, nine years younger. His father had been a hard drinker, though he had stopped drinking by the time I met him. Many years later, Larry referred to his father as an alcoholic, describing how his parents had fought when he was growing up. His family had faithfully gone to St. Joseph's Catholic Church until Larry was in his early teens, when his father determined that the parish priest did not live up to his expectations and they stopped going. Larry was the oldest child, and when he was eight years old his brother, who was two years younger than he, died.

I had grown up the youngest of seven children in a large

farmhouse that my father and brothers had built. My family belonged to a non-denominational church that met in homes. Sunday mornings and Wednesday evenings, we had church in our home. Alcohol, tobacco, dancing, all the things that go with the bar scene, were unacceptable. I continued to attend church for the first few months after we were married, but when we moved to another town, I just didn't connect with the church and quit going. I also had a sister who died as a child, but it was long before I was born.

FAMILY PLANNING

After a few years of marriage, we decided it was time to start a family. Although we didn't get pregnant right away, we didn't worry; we knew it would happen in God's time. Still, when the test was positive, we were very excited. Since this was years before home pregnancy tests, I had a friend in the lab at the hospital where I worked run a urine test for me. I will never forget the excitement I felt when the charge nurse from the night shift called about an hour after I left to tell me "The rabbit died". (Of course, no rabbit had actually died; she was referring to an old method of verifying pregnancy.) She told me it was time to start knitting booties.

We looked forward to having a child. Neither of us had any strong feeling about the sex of the child; we just prayed for a healthy baby. We had no reason to think otherwise; after all, I had 20 nieces and nephews, all of them healthy.

We had friends who were also planning families, and life was good. When good friends found out that their daughter was anacephalic, we were devastated along with them. But in the back of my mind a little voice was saying, "This increases your odds of having a healthy baby."

The pregnancy was textbook perfect. Six weeks of mild nausea stopped right at the end of the third month. I felt life at about five months. I experienced a little back pain, but some chronic back pain was the norm for me. Then we had a quick delivery; after only six hours of labor, Anna Laura Raymer was born. We called her Laurie. It seemed more fitting a name for such a beautiful girl.

With her name, we honored our strong family ties. She was named after all four Great Grandmothers with just those two names. And after choosing the name, my mother reminded me that I had a cousin named Anna Laura. I had forgotten because, like Laurie, she did not go by her real name; to me, she was "Bobbie".

Laurie was a healthy child. She didn't have colds, allergies, stomachaches or any of the multitudes of other small health concerns that are common to most children. So when she spiked a high fever and complained of knee pain when she was three, illness was a new experience for all of us. We took her to the doctor, who found nothing wrong with the knee, but gave her antibiotics for the fever. When she quickly recovered, we went back to our usual routines.

We were busy with life. I worked as an Infusion nurse at the local hospital two or three days per week, Larry went to work for a short line railroad and we spent time with family and friends. If anyone had asked me, I would have said I was Christian, but I wasn't going to church and I didn't always live as a Christian should.

During this time, I think Larry was trying to sort out his beliefs. When I met him he had been only a few days back in the USA from Vietnam. He didn't talk about his war experiences very much in those years. What he did talk about was the good times, hanging out with his buddies, drinking too much and R & R in Hong Kong. Post-Traumatic Stress Disorder (PTSD) was not commonly talked about at that time, but I learned to live with it. It was not until years later, when the studies of Vietnam returnees became news that I was able to understand what was happening. I remember lying in bed frightened because Larry had stormed out of the house at three in the morning in the pouring rain to walk for hours. I remember fists and feet through walls and doors, the classic rages of PTSD.

Over the years, he was able to open up a little, to tell me stories about seeing men under his leadership die, seeing children die, seeing a friend, a pastor, die, having all but four men in his platoon die.

He was angry with God. He did not understand how God, as he understood Him, could allow these things to happen. The kind, caring, gentle soul that he was could not reason it away.

Because he had lost his ties to the Catholic Church, he no longer had that avenue of help. He was questioning, searching, and looking at his heritage. His father was part Native American and had honored his heritage with long black braids when Larry was young. Larry remembered feeling the pain of being called half-breed. He had learned about the culture, some of the beliefs of his people, but had never participated in any ceremonies, in part because he was too "White".

Counseling, either by a priest or shaman or psychologist, was never really discussed. I used what limited skills I had learned in nursing school to try to help him through the worst times of PTSD, even without really understanding what was happening. Things got better; the bursts of anger got further apart and less violent. I was no longer afraid, just irritated when he lost his temper.

We did talk periodically about our faith and our beliefs during those years, but it was not a priority in our lives.

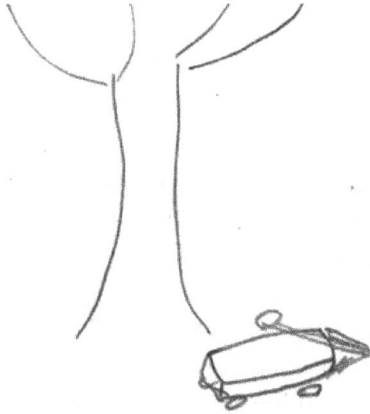

THE FIRST SYMPTOMS OF TROUBLE

Life drifted along, and we decided it was time to think about having another child. Again, it took about nine months before I got pregnant, no hurry, no worries. Several months had passed since Laurie had complained of knee pain.

Laurie was an active child, running and playing outside with her friends and her dog. She was very outgoing, always in the middle of anything that was happening. She was a natural leader, easily getting other children, even those older than herself, to do whatever she wanted without being demanding. At one family gathering, she was the one organizing her older cousins to play games.

Then in April of 1975, Laurie began to complain of back pain after she jumped off a wagon. It got better.

We were so excited when we found out I was pregnant again. When we came home after an evening out in July to find that Laurie was running a high fever again and complaining of knee pain, we were concerned, but not afraid. We took her to the emergency room, where they took x-rays and put her on antibiotics for the fever again. Nothing showed in the x-rays.

The fever went away, but she began to run less, and continued to complain of pain after the fever was gone. The pain was in her back again. Still, nothing showed on x-ray. It was late summer.

When Dr. Mason, her pediatrician, started listing the things that he didn't think it was, he mentioned CANCER. Even as a nurse, cancer had never crossed my mind. Children did not get cancer. That was an old person's disease. So I was shocked to think he was even thinking it was a possibility. But I didn't like the diagnosis he chose first either. Rheumatoid arthritis was still an old person's disease, but it was treatable and it was not terminal. So we started with aspirin for the pain and inflammation.

We took Laurie to a carnival that summer. We rode the Parachutes ride. She loved being up in the air where she could see so far, but she was still hurting. Because she could not walk far without pain, we put her in the wagon she had jumped from, using it as a stroller.

When Laurie stopped walking Dr. Mason sent her to an orthopedic specialist. His x-rays were very different; there was not just one area of concern, but many. Dr Bump, the orthopedic specialist, was sure he knew the diagnosis. He started her on Leukaran, an oral medication, gave us information about the disease, histocytosis, and asked us to have a biopsy done.

While she was in the hospital for the tests, Laurie missed her dog. Twinkles was too big to sneak into the hospital, but her puppies were still very small. We put the smallest one in a brown paper lunch sack and snuck her in to visit. Laurie loved it. The secrecy added a little excitement to the adventure.

The doctor made a "turtle shell" splint to help support and stabilize her back to reduce the pain. It met with limited success.

The first indication that there was something very wrong was when we got the first pathology report. The hospital pathologist found cells consistent with Ewing's Sarcoma but the clinical pattern was all wrong. Ewing's Sarcoma is a bone cancer, characterized by a focal tumor, usually in one of the long bones. The child is usually older, even in the teens. There is often spread to lungs and brain by the time of the diagnosis. Laurie was five years old, her tumors were spread throughout her bones, not just the long bones and she had no evidence of spread outside of the bones.

The decision was made to send the slides to the Mayo Clinic for review, hoping to get a clear diagnosis. The report returned probable Ewing's Sarcoma. That little voice I had heard years before came back to haunt me. I wondered if God was punishing me for finding good in someone else's tragedy.

And so began our journey through hell. Everything changed.

THE TREATMENT

We had been planning to take a trip to Hawaii that fall to celebrate our eighth wedding anniversary. It was something we had talked about doing for years, and the time seemed right to go. I had never been to Hawaii. Although Larry had been transferred to Schofield Barracks on Oahu a few months after we were married, we decided that I would go back to nursing school instead of going with him. My parents planned to travel with us. Instead, we spent that anniversary at Doernbecher's Hospital on "Pill Hill" in Portland, Oregon.

Doernbecher's is a children's hospital, part of the large complex of hospitals that make up the Oregon Health Sciences University. A tertiary medical center for much of the Pacific Northwest, OHSU is also a research center.

Dr. Mason arranged for us to be met in the lobby of the hospital by the Pediatric Oncology Fellow. It was a new world with new words; oncology and fellowship. I was torn between intellectual curiosity about all of the new things I was learning and fear for my child. Dr. Robert Neerhout, a pediatric oncologist, introduced us to the world of cancer research, protocols and chemotherapy. I was an infusion nurse. I gave chemotherapy; I was familiar with its side effects and results. My reaction to my daughter being given chemotherapy was very different than my reaction as a nurse. I was two people. The nurse understood the need for all of the tests; the mother hated the pain and the waiting. Frustration with long hours in waiting rooms resulted in many tears for both of us.

As the initial numbness of learning that Laurie had cancer began to wear off I reacted by wanting to know everything I could about the disease. I read everything that I could find on the disease, the treatment recommended, and the course of the disease. This set a pattern for how

I would deal with this painful period in my life. I did not turn to God for help, although there were certainly instinctive prayers at times of greatest distress.

Like King Asa in 2 Chronicles 16:12, 13 "...Though his disease was severe, even in his illness he did not seek help from the Lord, but only from the physicians. Then in the forty-first year of his reign Asa died and rested with his fathers."

My nursing education had been at a hospital school of nursing. In those days, most nurses were trained in hospitals, with as much importance given to practical experience as was given to theory. We worked in the hospital every morning until noon, then had class for two to three hours every afternoon. We had anatomy and physiology, microbiology, chemistry, pharmacology, and psychology, along with nursing arts. We learned that what we did was from a scientific base, what that base was and to question everything, but we did not learn much about the research process. When we graduated we were well trained in the daily routines of nursing.

That training helped me to understand to some degree what was happening to Laurie; however, the amount of knowledge about basic anatomy and physiology had advanced so far in the intervening ten years it was amazing. Cell functions that once were described in one paragraph now filled volumes. Even years later when I began to learn about AIDS, the variety of functions of those cells truly amazed me.

As David says in Ps 139:14, *"I am fearfully and wonderfully made."*

Because Ewing's Sarcoma is usually found in one focal tumor, amputation is often the treatment of choice, followed by chemotherapy, and sometimes radiation therapy. But Laurie had multiple lesions is many bones, including ribs, so that was not possible. We were left with chemotherapy.

The merry-go-round of home, clinic and hospital began. Laurie got her first chemotherapy treatment during her first hospitalization at Doernbecher's. One of the challenges of seeking treatment at a teaching hospital is that students do many of the treatments. Having been a student, I understand the need to build skills by practice. I support the practice. But it did not make it any easier to watch it happening to Laurie. It was one of the hardest things I have ever done to sit outside of my daughter's room, hearing her scream when they tried to start her

IV. It would be hard for any mother, but it was doubly hard for me because I knew that I could do it quickly and with much less pain.

They did not want me to start her IV because they thought that it might make her see me as one more person who hurt her. I believed that I would hurt her less. After repeated discussions with the doctors and nurses, I finally was allowed to start her IV. The rationale that finally allowed me to win that argument was that if she were diabetic I would be expected to learn to give her insulin. From that time on Laurie would not let anyone else start her IV. If an infusion needed to be started or restarted when I was not there, she would insist that they wait. "My Mom will start it when she gets here." I was also eventually allowed to give some of her chemotherapy at home rather than in the hospital for the drugs that did not require a great deal of fluid to be given with them.

One of the things that made our experience bearable was the wonderful staff at the hospital. They were sensitive to the other things in our life that were being affected. When we arrived at the hospital on the evening of our anniversary, we found a huge banner across Laurie's room that read "Happy Anniversary". Our anniversary had been forgotten amidst the many emotions we were experiencing as we started this journey.

During that time, I coped by pretending that life was normal. I continued to work a few days each week, along with keeping the clinic appointments, the hospital stays and attending support groups with other parents.

JOY

There were times of joy as well. I have wonderful memories of camping out at the beach with friends, flying kites, and chasing Laurie as she ran around the van we had. I remember family get-togethers with Laurie telling her cousins "Hey guys, I got an idea!"

One of my strongest memories of that time was of her creativity. At the time, her Uncle Lee was very involved in a Children's Art Show and Sale being held as a fund-raiser. Children were asked to enter paintings that were to be judged by local artists. Her Uncle Lee was a hobby artist and had done some lovely paintings that Laurie admired. So Laurie set out to do some paintings for Uncle Lee's show.

The show was held at Uncle Lee's store, Jacobsen's Burkhart's Florist, in Portland. Laurie's five paintings had been matted and hung with hundreds of others from children of all ages. When we arrived at the exhibit, we found local celebrities and a somewhat formal atmosphere. Laurie, who had lost her hair to chemotherapy, walked in, took off her knitted hat and announced clearly, "I don't have any hair." That was that. No questions, no funny looks, just a few laughs and she was content. She won an honorable mention and Uncle Lee bought two of her paintings.

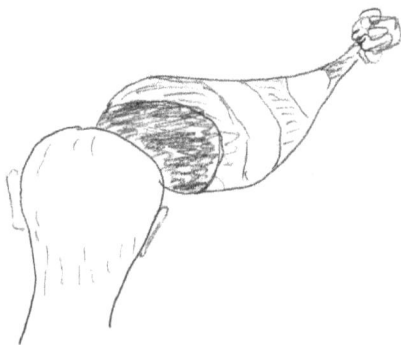

Laurie responded well to the chemotherapy at first. The lesions in her bones were no longer visible on x-ray. Her pain was gone and she was just a normal little girl, with no hair. We continued the chemotherapy, as the protocol was for 12 cycles.

Gretchen was born in March. Laurie was so excited to be a big sister! She went to the store and picked out a toy, a little bean bag lamb, for Gretchen and a little gift for Mommy in the hospital. I still have the little American Flag earrings that she gave me. Laurie loved Gretchen. A close friend reminded me recently that Laurie insisted on Gretchen's cradle being kept close to her.

RELAPSE

Then the pain returned, and we were back at the hospital with the endless rounds of tests. In late July, the doctors sat us down to discuss what they had found. Dr. Neerhout was very gentle. He explained the options. We could continue chemotherapy, but it was unlikely to work since she had relapsed while on chemotherapy. It was very unlikely that she would live very long, although he did not have a timeframe for us.

We chose to bring her home, with pain medication to try

to keep her as comfortable as possible. This was before Hospice, before the profusion of Home Health agencies. We tried to keep our routines as normal as possible. For a while, we had a wonderful pastor's wife coming to the house to watch the children on the days that I worked. But when she found out she was expecting twins her doctor told her not to work, so Grandma Raymer began caring for the girls.

I continued to work, for the insurance and to have some time away from the intense emotions. Those were hard days. With a four month old baby and dying four-year-old, there was little time to sleep. Sleep deprivation changes personalities; when patience was needed, tempers were short. I vividly remember dropping Laurie onto our waterbed one time when she was demanding to be moved. It was a drop of about six inches, nothing that would have hurt a normal child, but I'm sure it must have hurt her. It is one of the moments that haunt me still. I confess and ask forgiveness over and over.

Perhaps a week before Laurie died, we were talking about some plans and I said something about "when she was gone". She asked me, "Where am I going?" I didn't know how to respond. I knew that she was a bright child, but we had never talked about God or Jesus or heaven. She really had never experienced the death of anyone close to her. So I began to tell her about God, Jesus and heaven. I don't remember my exact words, but I remember saying, "Some people believe", not "I believe". I was not sure what I believed at that moment. I told her that when she was in heaven she wouldn't hurt any more, that she would be with God and Jesus. She listened without comment and seemed to be content with my answer.

Revelation 21:4 "He will wipe every tear from their eyes. There will be no more death or mourning or crying or pain..."

THE END

One morning Laurie asked me to lie down on her bed with her at 5:00 a.m. when I had had little sleep and was scheduled to work at 7:00 a.m. I asked, "When are you going to let me sleep?" She replied, "Don't worry Mom, you can sleep when I don't hurt anymore." I knew in that moment that she was prepared to die. I lay with her until she slept, then got ready for work. I told her good bye when I left.

That afternoon, Larry called me at work. I knew from

the sound of his voice that the time had come. He said I needed to come home. I told my coworkers and drove home. She was gone when I got there. Larry told me that she had complained that Gretchen was bugging her, so he had called his mother to come get Gretchen. Then he had been sitting with Laurie when she began to talk to him. She told him that some day he would find a friend. He started to tell her that he had me, but she stopped him. "No, I'm not talking about Mommy, I mean a very special friend." She then began to list all of the people she loved, and said, "I'm going to sleep now." Her breathing changed, and Larry went to call me. She died peacefully, thinking of the people she loved.

Larry and I both believe now that Laurie was telling him that one day he would find Jesus again. I cannot hear the hymn "What a friend we have in Jesus" without thinking of Laurie telling her father that he would someday find a very special friend.

Luke 10:21: *"and revealed them to the little children."*

When I got home, I checked to be certain that she had died, a very typical response from a nurse. I really had no idea what to do. I fell back on the things I would do in the hospital. I straightened the bedding, which did not need it, touched her face and smoothed her clothes.

I knew that Dr. Mason had been on vacation, but was due back at work the next morning. I called my friends on the pediatrics floor and asked for his home phone number. When I called his home, his wife answered the phone and told me he was on vacation. I told her I knew that and that I also knew he was due back the following day and explained the situation. She gave him the phone. I told him that Laurie had died and he offered to come to the house and to call the funeral home. We had stopped on the way home at one of the funeral chapels in town the day Dr. Neerhout had told us that Laurie was dying. Looking back, I wonder why; it seems so wrong. But at the time it was one of the things we needed to do to prepare. We had gotten information and talked about some of the things we wanted to do, so I was able to tell Dr. Mason whom to call. He came to the house and sat with us while we waited and took us out of the room while they removed her body from the house.

The tears come easily now as I write this, but then my eyes were dry, too numb to cry. I could talk about it, call the grandparents, and plan the funeral, but could not cry. With the help of family, I chose the dress she would wear, and her favorite soft afghan.

THE SCRIPT

One of the gifts God gave us during that time was a script. All my life I had heard the story of my sister, Ethel, my parent's second child. She was a beautiful girl with blond curls and a sunny disposition; the child everyone dreams of having.

When she was just three years old, Mother and Father were living on a farm in South Dakota, near Rapid City.

They had three other children, two girls and a new baby boy. Father took Ethel and her sisters with him out into the field to give Mother a chance to rest and care for the new baby. While in the field, Ethel stepped on a rattlesnake and was bitten two times in the leg. Daddy did everything he knew and packed her into the car to take her to the closest doctor. There was no antivenin in that office, so they headed into Rapid City, but it was too far away. They were unable to save her.

Despite the pain of losing a dearly loved child, my parents went on. They still had three other children and each other. In hearing the story through the years, I never heard either one blame the other, though I wonder now if they might have harbored such thoughts. If only Mother hadn't asked Daddy to take the older children to the field with him. If only Daddy had been more careful to watch where the children were playing. They each protected and supported the other's efforts; it was horrible enough without adding stress to their relationship.

I know that they were comforted by their faith in God. Their faith was their support, it gave them their support system and was the glue that kept them together.

They went on to have three more children and love one another until my father's death at age 80. I have often said that they did something right since I am the black sheep of the family and I didn't turn out too badly. It is not the things I have done that make me say that, but the things I haven't done. It is the years of forgetting God. It is the forgetting God's admonition to the children of Israel in Deuteronomy.

Deuteronomy 11:19, "Teach my words to your children, talking about them when you sit at home and when you walk along the road, when you lie down and when you get up."

Similarly, Larry's parents had suffered the loss of a child, which further served as an example for us in our time of pain. My husband Larry was the older of two boys. He and his brother David did everything together. Even then, Larry was quiet and David was his protector. I heard stories of David getting in a fight because someone threw Larry's cap in a mud puddle.

When David was six years old, he became ill. He had a bruised area on one leg that was thought to be the cause of a blood infection. When I heard this story, I began to wonder if he had leukemia, a tumor of the bone marrow.

The timing and symptoms were very alike. After six weeks in the hospital, in an oxygen tent, he died. This prompted his parents to review their lives. Larry's mother had been raised in the Lutheran Church. She converted to Catholicism, so that they could be married in the Church. Very soon thereafter they had another child, a girl this time and they stayed together until Dad's death at 65.

It is hard to look at this now and see how clearly we were given a script, the example of turning to God, yet we did not use that part of the script. The other parts, we used. We never blamed each other; we clung to each other, becoming closer, stronger as a couple.

We did talk about how our parents had responded. We talked about his mom's conversion and the family going to church. We talked about the fact that our parents had gone on to have more children while keeping the ones they had lost in their hearts.

At the time that Laurie was ill, I worked with two nurses who also had children with cancer. We often talked about our trials, how we felt, what it was doing to our lives. In both of their cases, the father had left the home; unable or unwilling to stay and face the day to day difficulties of having a sick child that might not live. I was so grateful that Larry stayed a part of our lives and actively participated in the necessary routines.

Also at that time one of the doctors I worked with had a child with severe brain damage. Sometimes we would talk about which was more difficult, losing a child to death or to a living death. It is a question to which there is no answer.

PLANNING THE FUNERAL

The Sunday afternoon that Laurie died, we began to gather our family around us. My parents came, Larry's parents were with us, and together, we planned a funeral. We all sat in a circle in the living room with the funeral director, discussing who would do the service, the music to be used and how we wanted it to be. Even coming from a large family, I had never experienced anything like this. Laurie was the first one in my family to be buried west of the Rocky Mountains. Because Larry and I didn't go to church, we had no one to ask. My parents were there, and offered to have one of the Workers from their church do the service. (Their church refers to their ministers as Workers. Paul refers to Timothy as "My fellow worker" and to Titus as "My partner and fellow worker." Rm. 16:21,2Co 8:23.) That was familiar to me, and Larry agreed. Then we had to pick music. I don't remember the hymn that was sung at the funeral, but I remember that we chose it because my mother had asked that it be sung. It was a hymn that had been sung at my sister, Ethel's, funeral.

I remember that the hymn was from the back of the hymnbook, so I recently went looking for it. I found there a little hymn that starts "Life at best is very brief" and ends with "God shall wipe all tears away in that grand eternal day." What a comforting thought that is now. Years later, when my mother died, we found a small cedar chest with hand made clothes that she had kept for over 60 years, a little apron with Ethel's name embroidered on it identifying them. I still have them.

Several of my nieces came over to help me prepare for the gathering after the funeral. I remember Donna teasing me about my "fly collection". I remember one of their husbands coming to take Larry out for a drive, keep him busy. I know it was painful for my niece's husband as well, as he had been there when Laurie was born and had watched her for us from time to time. My family was so important to me during that time.

I remember little about the actual funeral. I remember sitting in the family room with only a few tears, feeling guilty that I wasn't sobbing. I was still fairly numb.

One thing does stand out in my memory. The unit secretary and the play therapist from the hospital came to the funeral. It was very important to me to know that Laurie had had an impact outside of our family.

During those days I held onto Gretchen like a lifeline. Because I was nursing her, no one else could feed her. It was my time to focus on something other than death. I would hold her, rocking in the huge old Boston rocker we had, reveling in her health. As she grew older, I welcomed the colds and stomachaches. Because Laurie had had none of those, I felt it was a sign of a normal, healthy child.

BEGINNING TO HEAL

As the numbness began to wear off, I took time to say thank you to all those who had made such a difference to us. I sent flowers to a friend who had sat with Gretchen a few times while Laurie was in the hospital. I sent flowers to Betsy Mason for letting down the guard and giving the phone to Dr. Mason. He told me later that I got him in trouble; she wanted to know why he never sent her flowers! I took little thank you gifts to the staff at the hospital. It was a beginning.

The first two years were very difficult. Larry was very angry. He had lost so many people he was close to, his brother, his buddies in Viet Nam, now his daughter. He saw no purpose, no reason. How could a loving God do this to him? I don't recall anger. I remember saying "God has a purpose for everything; I just don't see it now. Someday I will." But I still wasn't feeling much of anything in those days, fearing that if I let myself feel I might fall apart, and I had to remain strong with a deeply grieving husband and a small child to care for.

One of the things that gave me comfort in the days following her death was that I was able to protect her from the pain of the IVs.

During those first days and weeks after Laurie's death, there was one thing that took me by surprise. We as Christians, often talk about family and friends who have gone before as watching over us. Physical love was always an important part of our marriage. It was a distraction from pain. We used to joke that Larry had a cure for my headaches. It was a bond, drawing us closer. It was joy in its intensity. But after Laurie died I found myself being inhibited by thoughts that she was watching us. It took some time before sex became a comfortable and comforting part of our lives again.

We discussed having another baby. We weren't sure if we were willing to chance the pain of possibly losing another child, but we didn't want Gretchen to be an only child. Finally, we decided to try. It had taken us about nine months both times before, so we thought it would take a few months again.

I got pregnant almost immediately. I told Larry that I wasn't sure if we made the decision or God just let us think we did. After Gabriel was born, life went on. There was work, school for the kids and more school for me. Even our terrible loss was not enough to wake us up to the need for regular fellowship and reading the Word of God.

I love to read. I read novels, history, magazines, and anything else that I can find. One morning about two years after Laurie's death I picked up a new book to read. The name of the book was "Six Weeks". It was later made into a movie, starring Mary Tyler Moore and Dudley Moore. It is the story of a young girl, given six weeks to live, who decides to do something important during the time she has left. I got two pages into the book when I finally broke down. I found myself sitting on my kitchen floor, sobbing. All the pain I had pushed down for nearly three years came gushing out. No more hiding behind the busyness of taking care of young children or trying to keep things together because I thought if I didn't Larry wouldn't make it. I was not aware of what Gretchen and Gabriel were doing while I was there on the floor. It was the only time I truly cried for Laurie. Then I buttoned it back up again. I never did finish the book or see the movie.

After that time, I often thought there was something wrong with me. I didn't feel things deeply as others did. I rarely cried over things that affected me, but would cry at movies, books, touching stories. I would hear people talk about how something horrified them and I would feel intrigued or disgusted, but nothing like horror.

When Gabriel was about two, I took a job on an oncology unit. I took a series of classes on Oncology Nursing, a program based on the Yale School of Nursing Oncology Master Program. Much of what I learned was helpful to me personally, in particular the classes on bereavement and grief. And I found that it was comforting to be able to help others through the difficulties of cancer treatment.

I had learned a new respect for my profession during Laurie's illness. It was the nursing staff that made all the difference in Laurie's care. She had marvelous doctors, but they weren't there all the time. The nurses dealt with the pain and fear and kept Laurie's spirits up with activities. To be able to learn those skills and give back some of the gifts they had given me was truly a blessing.

When people would comment about my profession, it was invariably, "Oh isn't it terrible to work with dying people all the time?" My response was usually something to the effect that I got much more than I gave. It was so life affirming to watch family relationships heal, to see people hanging on to say goodbye to a loved child or friend before they died.

During Laurie's last days, we spent hours watching the birds in the apple trees in the front yard, counting seven different bird species in a half hour time one afternoon. One thing I learned from my experience as an oncology nurse was to take life moment by moment. As a nurse, I learned to take pleasure in helping someone make it through eight or ten hours without pain, in calming fears, or giving 'permission' to cry or even to die. It was very gratifying to see the start of the Hospice programs. It would have been so nice during Laurie's illness to have had the support of a hospice nurse, social worker, and chaplain. I wonder if it might have helped us to see our way through the pain, back to God, much earlier than we did.

LEARNING FROM OUR CHILDREN

One evening when Gretchen was in her early teens she came home from a Christian youth night club and announced that she was saved. My response was to ask her what she thought that meant. It seemed so sudden; I could not imagine that she had any real understanding. Larry and I had always said that we wanted the kids to make up their own minds without pressure from us. That was our excuse for not taking them to church, or teaching them about our faith.

Gretchen began to go to a Four Square Church with a friend, and was baptized there. She asked me to go. While I was there, someone began speaking in tongues. It seemed so strange to me, like a made-up language. I never went back. Thinking of it now, I am reminded of Paul's teaching in 1 Corinthians 14:23 about the gift of tongues. I did think they were crazy!

But true to our plan, I tried to not discourage her from going to church. Several years later, she married the friend who had taken her to church. Gretchen and Jesse LaDeane were married in a little church across the street from where she went to elementary school, just thirty years and three days after Larry and I were married.

About that time, Gabriel started seeing a Mormon girl. Again, I was not pleased, but did not interfere. When we talked about his newfound faith, he said that the most important thing was faith in Jesus as the Son of God and our savior. Gabe married Susan Hamilton just one year out of high school.

Then we began to have grandchildren. When the second one was born, we drove back to South Dakota, where Gabriel was stationed in the Air Force, to see him. It is a long drive with lots of time to talk. Somewhere in that long trip Larry said "I think we need to start going to church." My response was immediate. "OK, where?" Our upbringing was so different; it was a legitimate question. We discussed options and finally chose the community church where Gretchen and Jesse had been married. It seemed to be neutral ground and we knew the pastor. So that Mother's day we went to our first service.

It was a new experience for both of us; it was not the formal, structured service that we were familiar with. More charismatic, the congregation stood and clapped or raised their hands, swayed to the music. And the music! There were guitars, drums, piano, organ and sax. After more than 30 years with only rare attendance at church services, things had changed, it seemed. I loved it.

NEW HEALING

I had been feeling more and more that I didn't experience emotions the way others did. But I would sit in church and cry through the sermon. Larry would ask me what about the sermon made me cry and I couldn't answer him. I had told him that I watched sad movies to cry so that I didn't have to cry for myself. I thought that maybe I was now using the church the same way.

For years, I thought about how I felt about going to church. I missed the social aspect of church, but as time went by I found that I had a deeper faith in God. After we began to go to church again, I found myself focusing on my faith. One instructor in a class I took said that you fall in love with what you focus on. I found myself falling in love with God. I began by getting up a little earlier each morning to spend time in The Word and in prayer. I soon found that I was jealous of that time; when family or work interrupted my devotions, I was angry.

Then one spring, I went to the Women's Retreat. It was an experience that I will never forget. One evening the guest speaker was telling of an experience when she had been told by someone that Satan had her heart bound up, that she saw bindings on her heart. That was why she was depressed and angry. Of course, they prayed with her and the bindings were released and she felt much better. I was still pretty skeptical in those days about modern miracles and hearing the direct word of God. I believed in Jesus, that He was our savior, but didn't really believe that he intervened in the here and now.

Later that evening, when she was praying for individuals and we were all holding hands, I had a vision of strips of cloth wrapped around my heart. I prayed that God would remove the bindings that I might be able to truly feel the emotions that I had faked so well for so long.

At that moment, I felt and heard a strong tearing sensation in my chest. It was so strong that I jumped and almost dropped the hands I was holding. It was not painful, but very distinct. I began to cry. From that time on, I have felt more intense emotions, more true compassion. It is subtle, and not likely noticeable to those who know me, but I feel it.

I still have my own stash of Laurie's things. When Gretchen's daughter was born, I opened the box for the first time in many years to take out a pretty yellow afghan that Grandma Raymer had made for Laurie. It was time to pass something on to the next generation of children.

When Gabriel, now in the Air Force, was sent to Saudi Arabia with war in Iraq looming, I dug out the little flag earrings. I didn't wear them, but somehow, they were a comfort to me, a little thread of connection between Laurie and Gabriel.

THE GIFTS

One of the changes that occurred over these past few years was an awareness of the gifts that God has given me. Most of all, He has given me His love and patience. Through all the years of ignoring Him, He never gave up. He invited me over and over. He did not turn away when I did not respond.

He gave me a loving family who know and worship Him. Growing up in a home where the bible was read daily and I often found my mother or father on their knees in prayer gave me a steady foundation to build on. It was something that I did not truly appreciate at the time. Many years later, when my brothers and sisters got together to celebrate my Mother's birthday, one of my brothers said that we didn't know how lucky we were in our parents. I could honestly say that I truly did.

He chose a husband for me who has been my anchor. I can not imagine what my life would be without Larry. He has always been there to talk to about anything I was willing to bring out in the open. He was honest and open about his own feelings, letting me see deep in his heart. Since returning to God's church, I have worked at being a better wife to him. Perhaps because of spending a year with nothing in my life under my control, I have always wanted to be in control. I struggle to give that control up. First to Larry, as my husband, that I may give God control over my life.

God has given me the gift of knowing that my children love him and that of knowing that my grandchildren will be raised knowing him.

Both Gretchen and Gabriel have grown into wonderful adults. They are caring parents who do their best to teach their children about the saving grace of our Lord.

They also have a connection to a sister that they never knew.

Laurie is buried with her Uncle David and Great Grandma Raymer in a cemetery just a few blocks from where Gretchen and Gabriel spent their teenage years. Both of them visited her grave. One of the gifts that God gave me was a wonderful mother-in-law. She took me with her to clean the family graves, something that I passed on to my children. It was a ritual to clean the graves on Memorial Day. But they also visited in times of stress or joy. They each have told me that they would sit on her grave and talk to her.

And there was one more connection. When they married, Uncle Lee gave each of them one of the paintings that he had purchased at the Children's Art Show and Sale. Both of them hang them proudly on their walls, a reminder of a sister they didn't get a chance to know, except through the stories they heard from us.

As I said at the beginning, I don't have all the answers. I do not pretend to know anything about doctrine. I listen to discussions or read books that give conflicting interpretations of the bible. Some believe that the Bible is a very literal pattern that must be followed exactly. Some believe that it is less literal, more a guide. I am inclined to believe that there are a few key truths and most of the rest is revealed to each one of us as we need it.

When Jesus healed the boy of an evil spirit in Mark 9:29 the disciples asked him why they couldn't cast out the evil spirit? He replied, "This kind can come out only by prayer."' Even in His earthly ministry there was not a set formula. Each situation was handled differently, based on those few absolute truths. Also in that passage, when Jesus told the father that if he believed, he would heal the boy. The father's response was "I believe, help me with my unbelief". I so relate to that feeling.

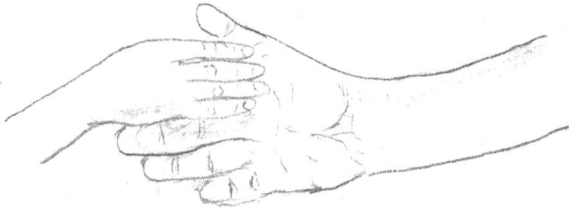

A SECOND CHANCE

God has given us a second chance. Where we failed our children, we have the new opportunity with our grandchildren. God's word tells us in Deuteronomy 4:9 "Only be careful, and watch yourselves closely so that you do not forget the things your eyes have seen or let them slip from your heart as long as you live. Teach them to your children and to their children after them." Our children's children are too young to understand Laurie's story yet, but they are not too young to begin to learn about God and the sacrifice of his Son for our salvation.

God willingly gave us Jesus. In some ways, though our sacrifice was not willing, Laurie's death profoundly affected our salvation. What greater gift can we give our children and our children's children than the gift of the love of God?

AFTERWORD

A few years ago, I heard about a program called Parish Nursing. It is a specialty recognized by the American Nursing Association. A parish nurse is a registered nurse who has taken a basic parish nursing class and who works with the health ministry team. The parish nurse does not do "hands on" care or duplicate other available nursing or medical services, but seeks to creatively bridge the gaps identified in the health education and care delivery system.

The idea of an association between medicine and the church may seem new to some of us but scripture supports it.

In John 10:10 we read: *"I have come that you might have life, life in all its fullness."*

God's desire is that man should be whole. Healing is not meant to be confused with curing but is the restoration of wholeness, the process of becoming "whole" in body, mind and spirit.

God has given us a wonderful gift of life and it is our responsibility to keep ourselves well in body, mind, and spirit. Our good health enables us to have the energy and vitality to love and serve others. We praise and honor God when we use His gifts to work, serve others, and celebrate life.

The Parish Nurse extends a hand to individuals on the life long journey of physical, mental and spiritual health.

After much soul searching and prayer, I spoke with our pastor about learning to be a parish nurse for our church. He was very supportive of the idea. We now have an annual health fair/flu shot clinic and an annual blood drive at the church. The time I spend in the classes, planning the health fair and answering questions for individuals, has been a blessing to me. It has given me a much clearer vision of wholeness. I feel whole.

Oh, I feel the beginning of age, arthritis, sleep disturbances and other aches and pains. I still don't understand many things about my life. But I have come to see that they are truly connected. My body, mind and spirit are connected. What I do to one affects the others. If I keep my mind focused on God and my spirit raised to Him, my body is much better, if not perfect. It is when I focus on my body or my understanding that my spirit suffers.

After writing and rewriting this story, I finally let Larry read it. I did not want to print anything that was very different than his memory or that would cause him unnecessary pain.

He read this story on a week away, with no one watching for reaction and then asked that I include a little bit about his version of how Laurie reacted to being in the hospital. Being an outgoing child, she quickly made friends with other children who were in and out of the hospital at the same times she was. She knew who was very ill, and who lived far away and so had few visitors. That bothered her. She thought everyone should have visitors, so when Larry would arrive after work to visit with Laurie, she would insist that he put her in the wagon and take her to visit the children who did not have a parent or friend visiting them. These nightly rounds were painful for Larry.

For many years, the sight of a thin blonde child would bring Laurie back to him. Like Laurie, our oldest grandson was a born leader. When he was little, he especially brought Laurie back.

Larry carried, in his wallet, a snapshot of Laurie holding her helmet, standing in front of his motorcycle. It was faded, stained and tattered. Since reading this story, he has taken the picture out. I believe that reading my words have given him more healing as well. The picture will stay with us, a small reminder of a gift from God.

All Bible verses quoted are from the New International Version.

The descriptions of Parish Nursing are adapted from course materials and brochures provided by my instructors at the Northwest Parish Nurse Ministries.